Praise for *Dark 1*

"J.E. Stanley's poetry -- smooth and dark as espresso sipped in the secret jazz club of lost gods -- sweet haunting melancholy that gets under your skin and into your dreams like a beloved melody -- touched with exquisite sadness, and a dash of shiver, like blood drops in fresh snow -- read and savor."

Mary Turzillo,
author of *Your Cat & Other Space Aliens*

"J.E. Stanley is a blue-collar, rock-and-roll, sci-fi street poet throwing down words like the rumbling bass line on a garage-band redemption song. Don't just read these poems, listen to them. The music will make your mind dance all night."

Mark S. Kuhar,
author of "*e40th & pain*" and
"*acrobats in catapult twist*"

"If Cleveland were a medieval castle, J.E. Stanley would be the falconer, an eccentric man whose soul purpose in life is to take raw, young birds and train them as fierce killing machines, machines that can plummet through the air at a miniscule target, a goose or a pheasant, trapping it in their claws until it releases its life. This is because Stanley excels at the art of capture, and these poems stand as a testament to that art. Each one offers just enough to snag your emotions in the talons of the words and leave you with your feathers shuddering, breathless, yearning to surrender.".

Joshua Gage,
author of *Deep Cleveland Lenten Blues*

Dark Intervals

"Light is only precious during dark intervals"
-Keith Jarrett

For Rachel Kendall,
writer, poet and editor
extraordinaire!

J. E. Stanley

Professional Reading Series
vanZeno Press
Cleveland, Ohio

ISBN: 978-0-9789244-2-8

Cover Art: "Youth of a Nation" by Spyros Heniadis,
www.marinatingthemind.com
Cover Design: Heidi Della Pesca, www.nightship.net

For Joanne Cornelius, Lynn Luoma, my wife Diane, & my son Mike.

Table of Contents

1.

2.

3.

4.

5.

1.

The Renegades

We won't admit it, but it's already over, really.
Jesse's just gotten his draft notice. That's the worst of it.
And some Detroit band is trying to get a restraining order
saying that we can't be "The Renegades" because they're
"The Renegades" and they own the name.

And Dallas showed up drunk at the meeting in Chicago,
so now the album deal is gone.
And right after the meeting Billy lost it and laid into him.
Broke his nose before I pulled him off.
And you can't take something like that back,
so now we've got no drummer.

And today, the bus broke down just outside Porterville
so we're late and running on three hours of sleep
with nothing to eat but vending machine crackers
and no time for a sound check
and everybody edgy
and two dozen calls, but no substitute drummer.

Add the inevitable stage fright,
even in a small club like this one
and tonight's going to be a disaster.
But unlike the Titanic we don't even try to turn away.
Just hit the iceberg head on.
And yeah, will probably be our last gig.
Ever.
But it still matters.
It always matters.

A line of Jesse's keeps scrolling through my head:
"This whole sad world was born to bleed."

And now it's time to go on.
And (I can't believe it) Dallas shows up,
right eye black, blue, swollen. Nosed taped up.
He won't talk to any of us –
just goes to his drum kit and sits down.

And, Billy slides up to his opening note on the bass,
does his riff with perfect timing, perfect feeling.
Dallas comes in on drums,
right there with him,
right there, in the pocket.
Jesse chugging perfect rhythm on his Strat,
I hit the button on my Big Muff pedal,
and my old Gibson guitar does it's sweet and sour wail.
Jesse leans into the mic
and goes into "Lie to Me" with his trademark growl.

And everything's different now.
The air itself curved, electric.
Nothing exists but the music,
'cause *we're* The Renegades
and we will scream an "I Am,"
that breaks through this cage we call a universe.

And what if this whole sad world *was* born to bleed,
we're The Renegades
and we were born to rock.

Insomnia

3 a.m. purgatory.
Decaf and cigarettes
in "sammy jo's All-Nite Café."
Exterior of rust-streaked aluminum.
Scenic view of the rail yards.

I sit in the end booth
with its duct-taped seats,
my back, as always, to the wall.

At the far end,
three petty conspirators
with desperate eyes
plotting in hushed tones.
Probably headed for jail,
or worse.

The hooker from the 3rd floor of my building
complaining to the waitress about her rash.
The waitress, Tina
according to her faded nameplate,
not really listening,
her sad brown eyes focused somewhere
distant.

A trucker comes in
and plops down at the counter,
glances at the hooker,
maybe doing a mental tally
of what's left in his wallet
and how much of that he can spare.

"Island of Lost Souls," I think,
"Wasn't that the title of something?"
Not that I'm any different,
still lost myself,
even after three months back in the States.

Still, this little diner
is better than the small, bare room,
two doors down,
in the hotel with no name:
just "HOTEL" flashing on and off
in red "B" movie cliché neon.

The heavy locomotive rumble
invades my thoughts.
I should be on a train
headed back to Ohio.
At least Ohio is home
or was once.

Nothing to keep me here
except, of course,
that I don't know anyone here and,
more to the point,
no one knows me.

From the small radio behind the counter,
Bill Evans on piano
I close my eyes,
try to breathe the rhythm,
absorb the chord changes.

And maybe if I could sleep
through the night,
just once,
things would be clearer.
I could sort everything out.
If I could sleep.

FNG

Somewhere in the delta,
a place with no name,
under the unbearable weight
of an alien sun.

Thirst intensified
by acres of dirty rice paddy water.
Flimsy yellowish-green plants
offering no cover.

M-16 ready,
unless it jams
because it gets wet
or overheats
or you load a full clip into it.

The dense treeline ahead
like a wall,
perfect cover
for any sniper
or even the whole NVA
for all you know.

And you make a perfect target,
imagine a dozen AK-47's
trained on your right eye.

You heard that color-blindness
would make camouflage useless,
make snipers visible.
If only you could give up color,
even for the rest of your life.

And because you're the FNG
they make you walk point,
the first to die
if it goes bad.

FNG.
Fucking New Guy.
Target.
You.

Smoke and Mirrors

Talk, small and meaningless,
because nothing matters
except her eyes,
her lips,
her hips

and her hand
touching my arm.

Her breath
all tobacco and beer
and maybe
just one beer away
from lowering her standards,
just enough

for a night
with someone to hold,
a night to pretend,
to close her eyes,
make me some white
cliché knight,

while I tell myself
that maybe, just maybe
she'll stay
once the night is over,
once she's sober.

Each of us user
each of us used,
we lie to ourselves
for a brief human touch.
But in a night so long
in a world so hard
what other truth
can there be?

Maybe Next Year

At the Vietnam Veterans Memorial,
a girl, with her hands flat against the black wall,
eyes closed in concentration.
Long, straight, blond hair,
tie-dyed shirt and beads,
like a hippie, like me,
still lost somewhere back in the sixties.

She opens misty blue eyes,
sees me there,
speaks as if we were old friends,
instead of strangers.

"There are ghosts here," she says,
"I can feel them sometimes.
It's like communion."
Her hand brushes one of the names,
tentatively, reverently
· "That's my brother.
he's not here,
at least, not yet.
I come on this date every year.
To check.
He's not here.
Maybe,
maybe next year."

    And, I don't say:
    "But, there are no ghosts.
    What's gone is gone
    forever. Sacrificed,
    for rubber and rice,
    and the containment of imaginary dominos.
    And nothing can make it right.
    Nothing will ever make it right."
    No, I don't say that.

And now she's crying, softly.
So, I just hold her,
and say,
"Yeah, next year.
Maybe,
next year."

Search Party

Search the endless woods.
Spread out, call her name, listen.
Breath fogs the November air.
Cross the creek,
as dusk yields to rapid darkness.
Flashlight, extra batteries, ready.
Danny's sister,
missing.
"Don't worry," you tell him.
"We'll find her. It'll be OK."
You say it with confidence,
as if it were somehow up to you.

> You don't tell him about that other search party,
> all those years ago,
> before he moved here;
> He can't know
> how that ended.
> Three long days, two long nights,
> two bodies, one of them your older brother,
> the other his best friend.
> You keep that to yourself.

Spread out, call her name, listen.
While your mind lists possibilities:
Maybe, she just hitched a ride to Florida or someplace warm
on a reckless adventure,
or she's holed up at some friend's house a phone call away.
Maybe, she is wandering these woods,
and can be found. Found in time,

Spread out, call her name, listen.
And though you learned at 14
that even the most desperate of prayers,
will not break the silence of god,
you pray.
Sometimes, that's all you can do
call out into the darkness,
hope for an answer.

Flames

He wouldn't talk about Vietnam.
One night, after about two weeks,
he built a small campfire,
brought out his uniform
and threw it on the flames.

Fire to burn the memories of fire

I brought out a couple of beers,
sat there with him, silently
watching the hypnotic flames.

The moon had risen.
I remembered that, as a boy,
he wanted to be an astronaut.

I thought about the moon landing
that he didn't get to see,
about small steps
and giant leaps.

Austin

Hangin' out at the Mean-Eyed Cat:
Longhorn Lager, Frito Pie
and nothing but Johnny Cash
on the Continental AMI.
Eva, dark-eyed and brown-skinned,
oozes an animal sensuality in the sultry air
when, finally, we leave the bar.
We don't make it out of the parking lot –
just make love in the back of the old pickup.
Later, we lie on worn sleeping bags,
trying to count stars and, damn,
the night sky really is deeper
and brighter in Texas.

Albedo .07
inspired by Mary O'Malley's "White Moon in Blue Sky"

Hide during daylight,
behind a mask
in a tenuous theater,
read lines,
play the role,
stay disguised.

Only the night is safe,
protected by the dark regions of the moon,
the sun's trespass
reduced to a minute fraction
of its incident light,
the shadows deeper and cooler.

Even blood spilt on the whitest snow
would not be red,
no matter how deep the cut.
Everything reduced
to shades of gray,
a safe monochrome unity.

Renegade Soul

My soul would be an outlaw
-Harlan Ellison

My soul, too, would be an outlaw,
an incorrigible renegade.

He is, of course, quite mad,
and not only confesses this madness,
but embraces it,
says that only a madman,
separated from the world,
can see it clearly.

He would
compose transcendental fugues,
paint eternal truths,
write of the rare gift of sentience
and see the world changed.
But I know that he will never find
the notes,
the colors,
the words.

I say he is merely a transitional animal
in the long chain of evolution.
He claims that that is the best thing to be,
part intellect, part beast,
son of earth, grandson of stars.

I argue that he is a fool,
question his very existence,
claim that he is nothing but 25 watts of errant electricity,
passing through synapses,
neuron to neuron
to neuron squared,
just one more set of cold equations.

But, silly old fool that he is,
he prattles on about the whole being more than the sum of its parts,
laughs at me,
and tells me to listen,
to the voice of the wind,
the silent eloquence of the desert.

Le Cercle Rouge

It has just begun.
Like midnight film noir:
a back street stakeout
on a rain-slick night.
It will not end well.
The detective already knows this.

The pivotal clues will be simple enough:
the timing of the gunshots,
the phone number penciled
on a matchbook
from *Le Cercle Rouge,*
the Polaroid hidden behind
the other photo in the antique frame,
the dark-haired girl in the picture,
piercing accusation in her eyes.

There will be
betrayal,
bloodshed,
shattered hearts
and finally,
the truth exposed
but, as always, with a price.

And when it's over,
no one
will be left
unscathed.

Aftermath

Pallbearer, yet again.
Flag-draped coffin
closed.
The marbled columns
framing the altar of St Mary's,
beige and purple,
as if of quarried stone
mixed with dried blood
sanded prematurely smooth
and polished
to an unnatural shine.

Rudolph

Here's the truth of it:

That foggy Christmas Eve never happened.
The harassment never stopped.
Rudolph might as well have been,
say, the only Jewish kid
in oh-so-gentile 1940's Porterville,

Once, after they tired of their reindeer games,
they cornered him in the playground.
He got in a few good hits of his own.
But, he was small
and severely outnumbered,
so they beat the shit out of him.

Even after Rudolph passed out,
Donner kept kicking him,
punctuating each kick with

"freak,"
"freak,"
"freak."

And, it wasn't just Rudolph's nose that was red.
His blood was red, too.

Juxtaposition

The hunter scanning
for the quick flash
of white-tailed deer.

The young wife
in her backyard
at the forest's edge.

Her white gloves.

Convergence

Not one double, but many.
A new you, an alternate world,
split off with every decision:

a you who ordered bacon instead of sausage for breakfast,
who caught that bus to Philly in '71,
who never married Catherine,
and on and on,
thousands, millions of distinct realities,

yet all leading to a single now,
this moment when it all implodes.
Back to one and only one you,
alone in a cheap motel room
on the outskirts of Basin City,
under the harsh light of a bare bulb
with a half-empty bottle of Jack,
a loaded .45
and no decisions left.

Yuki-Onna

Incarnate ghost of winter,
my final lover,
take what you will.

Flow through me,
with your crystallizing kiss:
your slow permafrost seduction,
a cold, numbing opiate.

But, as my final breath rises
through the barest of branches,
know this, Yuki-Onna,
whose feet leave no prints
in the crusted snow:

You did not find me
lost in your storm.
I sought, and found, you.

2.

Blues Song

like the naked trumpet
that echoes
through the alley, yearning
blue and deeper blue,
the first and last
and only sound
in this alone
night.

The naked moon
with no light of her own,
abandoned realm
of the huntress,
goddess of the wild,
now forsaken
in the concrete minds
of cold and modern
men.

The naked silence
of 3 a.m.
and I read to seduce
sleep, but the book
is James Morrow's
"City of Truth,"
disillusionment
laced with depression
when what I really need
is a convincing
lie.

The naked absence
of you with nothing left
but the black panties
from the hamper that you missed
when you packed,
and your scent
which draws me
again and again
to sweet and sour
loss.

Back Room Mood
with Joanne Cornelius

Under the cracked moon,
cold midnight light
falls blue on distant melodies.
Chimes of the Pleiades
illuminate the remnants
of safe harbors.
In the backroom
of Bearfield's,
hand drums beat out
dark Cleveland poems,
invoke d.a. levy
in dream rhythms
of the now born days,
smack harmonica pulses
into air pockets of peace
and being. Sing deep.
Sing deep.

at the end of words

the distance between us
   at the end of words,
speech locked away
   safe, keys melted down.

unforgiven moon
   all that shines,
the absent sun
   no longer missed.

a forced euclidean infinite.
   parallel lines
destined to yearn
   but never touch.

a thin veneer of normalcy
   courtesy ssri's and benzodiazepines
but, just for tonight,
   tell me it still matters.

lie if you have to.

Wilderness

Even out here, the silence speaks.
The wind breathes lost songs.
And the trees
whisper quiet stories
of sad human truths.

Whenever I See You, Even After All this Time
Inspired by Wanda Sobieska's "Segment of a Letter"

Extinguish a candle.

Then place a match
in the memory of smoke,
an inch or two above the wick.

The candle itself will re-light,
having no alternative
save a return
to its natural state

of burning.

Only the Moon

The sun pounds us down
with its August hammer.

The earth draws us back
to its womb of moistened dirt.

Stars wink and flirt
but from an impossible distance.

Only the moon
calls us to flight,

says "Come back.
Come back. I miss you."

3.

Lake Erie

so much depends
upon

the black leather
glove

frozen in february
ice

so far from
shore

Djam Karet

Ann said my poem was depressing
but, then again,
knowing me,
she didn't expect happy.

No past trauma
or repressed drama,
just brain chemistry
consistent with heritage, parentage,
one too many roads taken/not taken.

and my natural affinity for darkness,
the sunlight haunted
by a coven of ravens
always watching, impatient,
coveting my eyes.
Only at night,
when they are blinded by the moonlight
can I remain hidden.

Daytime requires protection,
a Bach fugue, a Tarantino film,
the poetry gypsy in her red raincoat
dancing electric wordstreams,
anything divorced from time and space,
providing the illusion of infinity
within the solitary second.

Words
by Joanne Cornelius & J.E. Stanley

Her lips and eyes don't lend to words.
This alchemy transcends my words.

As distant worlds burn in her eyes,
she steels their flame to blend with words

The future bends back and curves to now:
just new beginnings, no end of words.

The desert moon shines in her sky
as Ofra's prayers ascend on words.

Liquid lines ooze and flow at will.
No poet ever penned these words.

collage

one of d.a. levy's
with a naked woman
in the center
and everything else just
disappears

the camels
six of hearts
lucky seven social club
eagle stamp
everything
gone
the man she is straddling
gone
all the other women in the piece
even the topless woman
with her arm around
the other topless woman
gone

nothing left but that one woman
it's as if you'd never seen
a naked woman before
there's just something compelling
about her
this particular woman
and it's the same for everyone
if they've seen this collage
they haven't seen it
not the whole anyway, just

that woman
that naked woman
that nude woman
that woman
that woman

Prophet

for Joshua Gage
with Joanne Cornelius

Wild gazelles,
cloaked in rhyme,
run free,
and fear no lion.

The prophet dons his purple robe,
nails his palms to the stars
with his pen, emerges
from the echinoid Cuyahoga
though clouds of steel smoke.

He sings the gospel
of Brew Kettle beer,
coffee and cigarettes,
Kerouac, U2,
the word and the Word
and the woman.

And though at times
skeptical and hesitant,
our hearts
sequestered
behind kevlar vests
and walls of quarried stone,
sometimes,
we listen.
Sometimes,
we hear.

river man
for Dan Smith

in hemingway's panama hat,
with garcia lorca's guitar slung on his back,
he walks the arteries of the city,
collecting jigsaw fragments of its essence:

strontium 90 bled from the old bones
of mimeographic ghosts,

a handful of fire
from the burning cuyahoga,

trainwreck radio soundbites
thrown against a pollock canvas,

scrap metal blast-furnace tears
alloyed with coppery hues
mined from lake erie sunsets.

he assembles all of it
into a pyschotropic collage,
the past and present
of a forsaken, rust-belt cleveland,
the mirror of a city's evanescence.

Poetry reading orgy
with Joanne Cornelius

I suggest a duo
she considers a threesome
we laugh / his neurons
flash sharp images
electric siren songs
impossible menage explosions
of sudden criminal beauty

in an awkward
Bearfield court
startled syllables
spark poetic fragments
raw words intertwine
capture lines
in spontaneous seduction
instant combustion

we tread overhead
fingers travel quickly
through pages burning
hot with soul-bared ink

contemplating duties
intimidated by mic
but true to selves
our charge firmly set
the sacred dance begins
elemental rhythms
brought to life
in primal
heart
beat
pulse

words once sheepish
now feverish
rush
one on top
of the other

she goes
he goes
she goes
they all go

synchronized lovely sounds
bleed through
this reading

these three virgins
freed

gypsy word dance
for Joanne Cornelius

cosmic neural explosions
burn electric pages
in virtual reality flash drive fantasies
and syncopated cerebral animal logic

stanza dam burst,
gypsy lips
call down the moon
to breed hurricane syllables,
underground adrenaline pyrotechnics
erupt into fiery star cities

full-throttle word surf
runaway thunder midnight special
shine, shine, shine
your light for me
set me free
set me free

If Dark Is What You Feel

If dark is what you feel
-- Liz Rosenberg

Words bleed out
in rivers of cliché,
but leave real stains
that will not be bleached.

Even after midnight's stark denouement,
shadowed by cold equations,
we cleave lines to fit Procrustean beds,
launch syntax into funnel clouds
of meaningless cacophony,
scatter syllables helter-skelter,
ream after ream

while bodies are piled at our doorsteps,
missing children remain missing,
and we deny the weight of the sky.
Confront its silence with mere noise:

our sole weapon,
our only solace,
transitory words
in bright and fiery song,

waiting to be lost.

Pollock's Canvas

Nothing
here is random.
Each molecule of paint
has dropped precisely where it needs
to be.

Ghazal to the Night

Enveloped in a purple haze all night,
the guitar renegade plays all night.

Beowulf is fiction, insubstantial myth.
Grendel roams free and slays all night.

In cloudless climes under starry skies,
lovers count the ways all night.

The holy celebrate rites of spring,
sacrifice virgins in praise all night.

The moon goes dark, forever gone,
leaves lonely distant stars ablaze all night.

Insomnia displaces troubled dreams:
the poet in deep malaise all night.

specific gravity

what *is* the *true* weight
of 21 grams?
a few scattered thoughts?

a 45 caliber round:
    chambered and impatient?
    airborne?

the weight of old poems,
devoid of music,
fed to the fire,
one by one?

of keloid memories,
sharply focused
in high contrast
silver nitrate images?

the weight of the rain sheeting the windshield,
    as I listen to Evanescence,
        and wait
for my wife to get out of church?

the weight of this page?
the weight
    of silence?

Ink
Art is a lie. . .
-- Pablo Picasso

This place is not of your time,
not of your world.

                        Here:

                                    Epiphany is real
                                    not temporary,
                                    evanescent
                                    delusion.

            Human voices do not wake us
            and we do not drown.

                        Darkness hides our faults.
                Even under the bright and naked moon,
                            we are free.

The small gods are left
solely to their own devices.
No human swords baptized
to holiness by infidel blood.

                                    And even if you cut me,
                                    I do not bleed.

            *   *   *   *   *

None of which is the least bit relevant.
The sole raison d'être of this fiction,
the most beautiful
and impossible
of lies:

In this world of Ink,
    I am the fairy tale Beast
        to your Beauty
            and you are in love
                with me.

4.

men of steel

post-industrial entropy
and erosion.

but, consider the bricks
laid by my grandfather
in decades long past-
still standing,
still strong.

consider the steel
forged by my brother
and father before him,
steel no super man
could ever hope
to bend
or break.

Tonight

Just "call me Ishmael tonight."
I read only Shahid tonight.

Beowulf returns from myth.
Grendel will not feed tonight.

"I am...Shiva...destroyer of worlds."
Mass times squared light speed tonight.

Man's explorations will not cease.
We orbit Ganymede tonight.

Nothing will grow save moon blue flowers
in dark gardens she will seed tonight.

All eight moons destroyed but one,
only the poets bleed tonight.

surfing the ruins
for and from Mark S. Kuhar

chippewa coaster surf,
waves of words crash
through cliff walls
of status quo static,

water to fire,
fire to light,

the ghost of garcia lorca invoked
in ohio dust
as distant church bells
echo the cry of the guitar
through desolate urban skies.

siren sing paeans
to lost city angels,
anthems of subterranean cuyahoga
drumbang hearts that
beat, beat, beat and wail

to the humbucking rock
and magnetic roll
of deep surreal blues.

cleveland in e minor.

Cleveland Cinquain

for & from Joanne Cornelius

1. Aluminum

Over
Bearfield's coffee,
from seeds of foil and ice,
she weaves complete and bright new worlds
with words.

2. Communion

Sacred
beauty defined.
Twenty-seven hundred
Clevelanders await the sunrise,
naked.

3. Sound Waves

This air.
These four voices.
united in one breath,
send prayers to the four sacred winds.
This air.

Cleveland Uncovered
1. the winds we ride
for and from d.a. levy

in this sad cleveland
that gave you nothing,
took everything,
"through the endless
days of rain and fire"
we gather, still,
to voice your words.

we shout
to the sky and universe within
that energy equals
dream
times the speed of light
squared.

let others embrace
convenient delusions,
follow savage voices
into the alone night.
we will scream to the sun
that civilized evil
is evil nonetheless
and we do not bow
to the hollow-point myth
of the machine savior.

the tombstone,
you once said,
is a lonely charm,
but know this:
the days unborn are here,
your sisters are here,
your brothers are here
and armed,

your dreams
the wind
that we ride.

Cleveland Uncovered
2. lady in red
for joanne cornelius

she spreads her palms
to reveal dominique's red,
red roses
thriving in ohio snow.

"eyes full of stars,"
she wears a red raincoat
in dry weather,
covers walls with posters of
levy & lennon
levy & zappa
levy & patti

and thirteen buddhist third
class
junkmail
oracle
security blanket,
life-saving
covers.

she jams with the fugs
in the flaming glow
of pre-steel lava,

pulls a bright red sun
from her pocket
to heal our skies
with her electric dreams.

Pilgrimage
for Joss & Summer

Those few of us still left
now follow this young girl,
in peace as we did in battle,
our own *Jeanne d'Arc*,
our own River Tam.

South across the water
to the shores of our origin,
the birthplace of our tribe,
the city-that-was,
now lying in ruins
at the mouth of the crooked river.

At her behest,
I wade deep into Erie,
surrender my ancient sword
to Lady Vivienne of the Lakes.

At nightfall, we gather on the banks
of the Cuyahoga,
throw our torches
onto the oil-slick surface
while she falls to her knees,
says a prayer
to Our Lady of the Burning River
and sees visions in the fire:
Cleaveland-that-was
and the Cleveland that could have been,
now lost.

I see only flame
but believe every word.

Cuyahoga River Blues

This river my life
winds,
bends,
exiled to aimless wandering
(no straight canal path conceivable).
Constant current
perpetually seeking
some elusive,
undefined
completion.

Water, waste,
polluted by life,
imprisoned by valley
and riverbed.
High ground,
visible,
inaccessible,
impossible.

Burning
with molten steel heat
in brief
and shallow flame.

No chosen destination,
arrival anywhere
solely by accident.

Slow descent the only constant.

This crooked river,
this aimless life.

5.

Ethics 101: Why the Mona Lisa Smiles
Inspired by Linda Pastan's "Ethics"

A hypothetical fire rages
through an imagined museum.

A priceless painting.
An old woman with a badly sprained ankle.
You can save one of them,
but only one.

And so, you choose,
the obvious choice.

Later on, you can tell yourself you did it for Art,
for posterity,
for the future of humanity,
and not for any reward
or on the off chance that
in the confusion of the fire
you can slink away unnoticed;
trade Miss Mona for a quick black market million.

And if you're really smart,
check the woman's purse for money.
$42 and change. And why not?
She won't be needing it.

Odds are, you'll look back on this day without regret.

But maybe, just maybe,
in years to come,
you will dream of the woman:
the terror on her face,
her grip on your pant leg as she panics,
as she pleads with you,
"Please,
don't leave me like this. Please."

And maybe, just maybe,
long after midnight,
you will jolt awake
to the echo
of her screams
as she burns.

Language

we are all children of Jackson Pollock. . .chaotic mutants.
. . .from his mad wrist spun us
                                        -Patti Smith

Stereo pounds.
Sky jamming on "Hotta."
I test my solos
on my old Fender guitar,
humbucking pickups
slicing time and space.
Then I just play,
thrash distortion into vibrating walls
lose everything to electronic dissonance
but fragments of melody still bleed through
into coherence.

And say it is true:
that we are all Pollock paintings
spun from space into organic colors
over billions of years,
descendants of amino acids, nucleotides,
star-forged carbon. . .
sparked by lightning into DNA
and hypercubed into sentience,

right now, nothing matters
except the rock, the roll
and the pulse of the universe
given voice,
given thunder.

So be it.

medusa

perseus
in stone-
medusa smiles

hermes'
stolen scandals-
wings to speed her feet

athena awakens-
to the hiss
of snakes

You Can Always Tell

A dog
who's been beaten:
the forced wag of his tail,
the way he flinches and shrinks from
your hand.

Haiku

jazz
      chord changes
   seasons

*

couple in bed
back to back, but touching-
furnace kicks on

*

calm silence
of the moonlit path-
grendel catches your scent

*

mars shines bright
cries of slain legions
permeate the wind

Recurring Dream

I am a murderer.
I have no memory
of this murder.
The dream does not reveal
who, how, why.
It starts later:
with the sure knowledge that I will be caught,
the pervasive sense of impending doom,
the wait
for the knock on my door
and the wish that I hadn't done it,
that I could somehow take it back,
like words.

Upon waking, I tell myself
that it's nothing.
Just a dream,
after all.
But still,
the mood remains
and I listen
for that knock.

Politics

The robin assaults
the window. Again
and again, he attacks
his enemy, his
reflection.

Memorial Day

we were soldiers once…and young
-- Hal Moore

Mourning bells echo
through still skies.
Picnics and volleyball nets
mingle with flags, flowers
and the memory of freedom.

Parades crowd narrow streets
while forgotten ashes
fall like black snow,
the ghosts of Ia Drang lie silent,
and a wedding ring is returned
to a young widow.

Even as darkness falls,
one can't quite forget
the unique smell of death.
History is merely a fading memoir
and there is no tomorrow.

The Last of The Renegades

Nothing left now
but an old vinyl 45,
"Lie to Me"
backed with "Born to Bleed,"
and me.

We were The Renegades
and we were going to be stars.
We knew it. Held onto it
like a Truth.

And today,
buried on page 18 of the Cleveland Press,
Billy, knifed on 45th
in a bar fight that spilled out into the street.
We'd always known his temper
would get him into real trouble someday.
But we didn't know what to do about it.

Nine years ago, it was Dallas,
who took off for the West Coast
a year too late for the "Summer of Love."
Died with a needle still in his arm.
I'll never forget his sister's voice,
long distance sobbing
telling me it wouldn't have happened
if I'd gone with him like he wanted me to.

And Jesse in '70,
the first to die,
came home from 'Nam in a body bag.
I said goodbye
to a photo on a closed casket.

His mother came up and said,
"It should have been you.
This is your fault.
It should've been you.
He could've had a deferment.
He could've been in college,
Not singin' in some goddamn hippie band."

I ignored her
and just walked out, numb,
into the cold January night.
Her voice, now more of a scream, behind me.

"It should've been you."

I let her keep her anger.
I didn't tell her
that he'd always made his own decisions.
When he got his draft notice,
I tried to talk him into goin' to Canada.
We could've taken my uncle's boat.
Easy, a short trip across Erie to Port Stanley.
But he wouldn't do it.

But maybe she was right, in a way.
Maybe, it should have been me.
Jesse was the best of us
and when he died
the music died with him.

And I may be the only one left,
but Jesse,
Jesse was the last
of The Renegades.

Dark Intervals
Acknowledgments

Grateful acknowledgment is made to the following publications in which some of the poems in this collection, often in different versions, have previously appeared:

30/25ths Not Just Any Versiaries: "Albedo .07"
103: The Journal of the Image Warehouse: "Aluminum," "the end of words," "Renegade Soul" and "Smoke and Mirrors"
Amaze: The Cinquain Journal: "Pollock's Canvas"
ChiZine: "Djam Karet"
The Secret Life of a Deranged Poet / Cleveland Anthology of Poets: (New Kiev Publishing): "Flames"
deep cleveland broadside #23: "Cuyahoga River Blues"
deep cleveland junkmail oracle: "Back Room Mood," "Blues Song," "Cleveland Cinquain," "collage," "Cuyahoga River Blues," "lady in red," "Lake Erie," "Memorial Day," "Men of Steel," "Pilgrimage," "Poetry Reading Orgy," "Prophet," "Wilderness" and "the winds we ride"
deep cleveland postcard project: "Austin"
The Ghazal Page: "Tonight"
The Hessler Poetry & Prose Annual: "specific gravity"
Ink (Gypsy Lips Press): "If Dark Is What You Feel" and "Ink"
LYNX: "Ghazal to the Night," "jazz" and "Words"
MoonLit: "Language"
Scifaikuest: "calm silence" and "mars shines bright"
Sein und Werden: "Le Cercle Rouge," "Renegade Soul," "River Man" and "Yuki-Onna"
Speaking for the Dumb: Rants & Other Writings by Poets & Pubs (Green Panda Press): "collage" and "the winds we ride"

Three–Chord Poems: The Poetry of Rock & Roll (deep cleveland press): "The Renegades"

"Back Room Mood," "Cuyahoga River Blues," "the end of words," "Ghazal to the Night," "Insomnia," "Maybe Next Year," "Renegade Soul," "The Renegades," "Search Party" and "Smoke and Mirrors" appeared in the chapbook **Dissonance** (deep cleveland books).

Special Thanks to Joanne Cornelius for her kind permission to include the collaborative poems "Back Room Mood," "Poetry Reading Orgy," "Prophet" and "Words."

vanZeno Press

www.vanzenopress.com

Through our Professional Reading Series, vanZeno Press publishes fine books of poetry that our editorial board believes meet high standards of excellence and deserve to be published; poetry written by poets who are serious about their work, and who actively read or perform their work at poetry readings and other events.

If you're interested in submitting a manuscript or in learning more about our publishing process, please take a look at the vanZeno website and if you're still interested, please send an inquiry letter with a sample of 5-10 poems to editor@vanzenopress.com